I am Beautiful
Journal Affirmations for Girls

Elizabeth D. Gray

© 2015 Diego Beach Publishing

ISBN-10: 1512362778
ISBN-13: 978-1512362770

An Affirmation on its own is a powerful thing. However, flexing the muscle of an affirmation with the conscious expression of your own words, thoughts and experiences is a transformative thing. Use this affirmational journal to not only absorb the powerful messages in each affirmation, but to accentuate them tenfold by the expressions of your own creation.

I promise you
You are beautiful

CONTENTS

From The Inside Out

It comes from the inside out
My smile does
And in the moment I release it
As an expression of my joy
In that beautiful moment
I feel beautiful
I am lit up from within
I can't control it
And I don't want to
It is a release of sorts
It's me admitting to me
That I just can't help myself
I have to let that joy escape
And then there it is
For all the world to see
Perhaps it's widely thought
That we are most vulnerable
When we cry
But that is not what I believe
It is when I release
The truth of my joy
In the most undeniable way
That I feel
Vulnerable and beautiful
All at the same time
Because when I smile
It comes from the inside out
And in that moment
I am giving the world
A glimpse of my heart
And what could be
More beautiful than that?

❧ Notes ❧

❧ Notes ❧

❧ Notes ❧

I Am The Only One

What makes something
Beautiful in this world?
What do we prize most
When considering its worth?
There is a universal understanding
That the world treasures most
Those things of which
There is only one in existence
These most precious specimens
Identifiable only and always
For their exquisite individuality
We see the evidence all around us
The more unique an item
The more coveted it is
And based upon this fact alone
And acknowledging the undeniable truth
That I am the only one of me
I must rationally and soundly conclude
That I am beautiful

❧ Notes ❦

❧ Notes ❧

❧ Notes ❧

Those Who Know Me

I often get told that I am beautiful
By those who know me
And I have to admit
I haven't really
Taken it as a compliment
Probably because they're biased
They have to tell me
Because they want me
To feel good about myself
So I take it with a grain of salt
Until I realize something
When I'm in their shoes
And I complement someone I know well
I'm being totally sincere
Because I know them
I'm the perfect judge
I've seen them at their absolute worst
Witnessed them struggle
And emerge from struggle
So when I tell them they are beautiful
Nobody knows that truth better than me
And I want them to take it seriously
When I tell them they are beautiful
Because I mean it
And I know it
So when those who know me
Tell me I am beautiful
They deserve the same respect
As speakers of truth
So when those who know me
Tell me I am beautiful
I believe them

❧ Notes ❦

❧ Notes ❧

❧ Notes ❧

Breathe

I find a quiet place to sit alone
And close my eyes
Blocking out every sound around me
To focus only on the
Rhythm of my breathing
And in the stillness of the moment
I am in awe of the miracle
That is this body
The miracle that is me
And when I focus in this way
Conscious only of
The inspiration and expiration
Of life-giving oxygen
Into and out of my lungs
In this moment
I witness the perfect rhythm
Of this miraculous body
And when I go on to visualize
Oxygen enter my bloodstream
Flowing through my veins
I marvel at the wonder
Of this body of mine
Functioning in precise harmony
Every moment of the day
And the simple acknowledgment
Of the miracle of my physical being
Fills me with a new appreciation
Inspiring me to a live a life
Worthy of the miracle
That is this beautiful body

✥ Notes ✥

_____

_____

_____

_____

_____

_____

_____

_____

_____

_____

_____

_____

_____

_____

_____

_____

_____

_____

_____

_____

_____

_____

_____

_____

_____

_____

_____

_____

_____

❧ Notes ❧

❧ Notes ❧

_____
_____
_____
_____
_____
_____
_____
_____
_____
_____
_____
_____
_____
_____
_____
_____
_____
_____
_____
_____
_____
_____
_____
_____
_____
_____
_____
_____
_____

Cookie Cutter

They call them cookie cutter houses
Each looks the same as every other one
Like cookies cut from a mold
They are so similar
That it's difficult to tell them apart
The message seems to be
That each should appear
Exactly as the others
As though conformity
Equates to quality
But I am not
A cookie cutter girl
Who designs herself
To be like everybody else
I want to be like one of those houses
On an interesting street
That draws your attention
Because it is different in a way
That intrigues you
And makes you wish
You could take a peek inside
I don't want to build a house
That is so like the rest
That I can't even tell which is mine
I want to build something
Different than the rest
Because I am not
A cookie cutter girl

❧ Notes ❧

❧ Notes ❧

❧ Notes ❧

Through These Lenses

Like the lens of a camera
These eyes have seen extraordinary things
As the director of my own movie
I have taken the shots
The close-ups
I have watched a sunset
Fire the sky before my eyes
A blaze set out upon the horizon
More beautiful than any painting
More poignant than any cinematic display
I have borne witness to heartbreaking events
And even as the tears poured
These lenses captured
The depth and breadth of the moment
I saw beauty there despite the sadness
For every scene that makes us ache
Also makes us grow
I witnessed the birth of life
In all manner of ways
In the sprouting of a humble seed
And in the cries of a newborn baby
Like the camera's lens
I filtered these scenes
Through my own perspective
Colored the landscape
With my own lighting
Projecting my vision
Onto the screen of my life
Through these lenses
I have both witnessed
And created
Beauty

❧ Notes ❧

❧ Notes ❧

❧ Notes ❧

Energy

I have fallen in love
With the energy of others
Who have an ability to set me at ease
To bring out the best in me
The quality of their energy
Comforts those around them
The beauty of their energy
Is like fresh air upon the soul
And no matter what
Their physical appearance
Their gorgeous energy
Transforms all that they are
Into beautiful
I have had the privilege
Of knowing such people
They are my kind of beautiful
And I aspire
To cultivate within myself
A quality of energy
That uplifts and inspires others
So that no matter what
Becomes of my physical shape
Now or in the future
The beauty of my energy
Will shine through
That I might embody
That which I admire most
The intangible quality of good energy
My kind of beautiful

❧ Notes ❦

❧ Notes ❧

❧ Notes ❧

I Am Worthy

I am worthy
Of every good thing in life
Yes, me
I am worthy
It is clear that we
As the female gender
So often fall victim to the great lie
That we must be told
By someone other than ourselves
That we are worthy
And this most destructive fallacy
Has fooled us into accepting less than we deserve
Has prevented countless among us
From achieving our dreams
From speaking up in our own defense
From building a life of our dreams
From thriving
But the truth is
It was never about them
Nobody out there
Is endowed with the authority
To determine my worth
And today I am standing up for me
I am declaring with my loudest voice
From the deepest space of my being
That I am worthy of love
I am worthy of success
I am worthy of abundance
I am worthy of all good things
I don't have to wait for reassurance
I'm giving it to myself
Right now

❧ Notes ❧

Notes

❧ Notes ❧

Shine A Light

There's not a single human being
In the entire world
Who does not find fault
In some part of themselves
And maybe it is impossible to eliminate
Every single insecurity
But when we focus on our faults
We become our own enemy
There will always be things
We wish we could change
So what can be done?
How do we make peace
With the flaws we find in ourselves?
We accept them
And then we let them go
Turning instead
To shine a light
On the things we love about ourselves
We list them out
We acknowledge them
We celebrate them
We express gratitude for them
We shine our inner light
On the things we love about ourselves
And the more we practice
This love of self
The less important our flaws become
And those self criticisms
Fade away into shadows
As we shine a light away from them
And onto all of those things
That we love about ourselves

Notes

❧ Notes ❦

❧ Notes ❧

How Beautiful Feels

It is within no one else's hands
To determine what beauty is to me
Even a vast consensus of its definition
Will not sway me
And that is because you cannot
Put your finger on a feeling
And although the world
May be wrapped up in the debate
About what beautiful looks like
I am immensely more interested
In what beautiful feels like
And I am on a lifelong journey
To explore my own truth
Of how beautiful feels to me
I have found it mostly
In the simple things
I have felt beautiful
While embraced by the warmth of sunshine
In a moment of renewal after a haircut
While looking down at my painted toenails
In a barefoot stroll through soft grass
As a cool breeze brushed against my face
In the simple act of lotion rubbed onto my skin
While walking in the rain
When putting on a new pair of shoes
An undiscerning person
Might gloss over each of these
As uneventful, everyday events
But those persons are blind to the hidden treasure
Reaped from these simple, yet precious gifts
Which express in the most extraordinary way
How beautiful feels

✒ Notes ✒

❧ Notes ❧

❧ Notes ❦

Unbreakable

Take a look
At all the precious jewels of the world
Revered for their dazzling colors
These priceless nuggets of wealth
Existing in the natural world
Every hue of the rainbow
Represented in all its glory
We covet these gems
As our greatest possessions
Endeavoring to wear them
As a display of wealth and prosperity
Yet the greatest of these
Has no color at all
Formed deep within the Earth
It remains hidden for billions of years
Subjected to the indescribable pressures
Of the Earth itself
Before surfacing on land
By the epic force of volcanic eruptions
It is the diamond
The diamond has its humble beginning
Cultivated unseen for ages
Subjected to the harshest conditions imaginable
And having been shaped and fortified by its experiences
The diamond emerges from those great depths
With a beauty that outshines all others
And with an unbreakable quality
Of resilience and strength
It is from this example in nature
That I take my comfort
Knowing that all I am experiencing
Will leave me both beautiful and unbreakable

❧ Notes ❧

Notes

❧ Notes ❧

Vision

Anyone can have pretty eyes
But not everyone has vision
That is another thing entirely
Vision sets forth the promise
Of possibilities before you
Vision imagines a path ahead
When all avenues appear blocked
Vision ignites a fire within
Allowing you to knock down walls
Vision places you ahead of this moment
Providing a preview of future success
Vision sets aside all obstacles
Relegating them to the category of insignificant
Vision is the tool by which
You construct your own wings
And use them to fly
Vision fuels your ability
To create your own momentum
To lift yourself from
The circumstances of the present
And into a tomorrow
Designed by you
Vision is not a quitter
It is immutable
Reinventing itself eternally
To address every conceivable situation
So go ahead and tell me I have pretty eyes
I will smile and thank you
But anyone can have pretty eyes
And I myself
Would rather be known
For having vision

❧ Notes ❦

❧ Notes ❧

❧ Notes ❧

We Are

We are compassionate
We forge friendships
Strong enough to last a lifetime
We are inventors
Our innovations nudging the world forward
To a better tomorrow
We are healers
With the power to soothe scars so deep
We can scarcely see their depths
We are leaders
With backbones of steel
And an intellect
To solve the world's greatest problems
We are creators
The world is our canvass
And our lives are our art
We are resourceful
Finding a way forward
When all routes seem blocked
We are achievers
Meeting and surpassing
The goals set out before us
We are the peacemakers
In a world at war
We are the voices of reason
We are beautiful
For everything we are
We are

❧ Notes ❧

❧ Notes ❧

❧ Notes ❧

The Me I Used To Be

They told me to love myself
It was such simple advice
But they didn't tell me how
They told me that feeling beautiful
Was up to me
But I didn't know where to start
And then it occurred to me
That starting at the beginning
Was just what I should do
Starting with the me I used to be
Photographs in my mind
Of the child I once was
That precious little girl
Full of light and possibility
And looking into her eyes
I found compassion rising within me
I wanted to encourage her
I wanted her to know that she was loved
I wanted her know that she was worthy
I wanted to tell her she was beautiful
I wanted to counsel her to never give up
I wanted to wrap my arms around her
And never let her go
And that is how
I fell in love with me
That is how I found my beauty
I found it by starting with
The me I used to be

❧ Notes ❧

❧ Notes ❧

❧ Notes ❧

Deep Blue Sea

My heart is a deep blue sea
An entire ocean inside of me
Within those depths are found
Both darkness and light
In neither aspect do I drown
For my wellbeing lies not
With my own self judgments
But with acceptance for all that I am
The surface of the deep blue sea
Is a tumultuous place
With some spending
Entire lifetimes up there
Afraid to drown
They are battered
By the force of the waves
Never understanding that
In order to find peace
They must not be afraid to go deeper
For the only way to master life
In the deep blue sea
Is by the balance of existing
Not only on the surface of life
But also in those great depths
Existing for periods of time
Away from the chaos
Of the pelting waves
My heart is a deep blue sea
And it is beautiful
Not only where the sun shines
But also in the darkest depths
Of this deep blue sea

⯎ Notes ⯎

❧ Notes ❧

❧ Notes ❧

Sisters In The Sky

I have more than once
Looked up at a star-filled sky
And felt insignificant
My one life among billions
A speck of dust in comparison
To the vastness of the universe
I questioned the meaning of my existence
And then one day the answer came
As if in direct response
To this inner contemplation
It was a simple science lesson
But what it told me was astounding
I learned that forged within me
Are the very same atoms
That formed those billion stars
Those same lights in the sky
Under which I felt so insignificant
That simple lesson told me
That within me is the stuff of stars
And I looked again to the sky
Knowing that my life mattered no less
Than those glorious stars
The legacy of our existence
Is that we are all connected
The humble earthling girl
And the mighty burning star
Never again will I question
The importance of my existence
For the stars and I
Share an unbreakable bond
And I will forevermore see them as
My sisters in the sky

❧ Notes ❧

❧ Notes ❧

✨ Notes ✨

Girlhood

Don't let them tell you
What girlhood is
Because there are as many definitions
As there are people on the planet
And girlhood is
Whatever it means to you
You get to decide
Because you're the one living it
You don't have to fit in
To some little box
That somebody else has built
Their declaration of what it means
To be a girl
Spend less time worrying about
What they think
And more time on
What you think
Be the kind of girl
You want to be
And hang onto that
For the rest of your life
At every age
Be fearless as you live a life
Of your own choosing
For the act of embracing
Your unique brand
Of individuality
Is a beautiful thing

❧ Notes ❧

❧ Notes ❧

ও Notes ও

Invisible Me

What you see when you look at me
Doesn't really tell you who I am
And that's the trouble
With the world today
People think they know me
But they barely scratch the surface
They'll never understand
Unless they get to know
The invisible me
You can't tell who she is
From the clothes she wears
The color of her skin
The eloquence of her speech
The grace of her walk
The home she lives in
The car in which she rides
The weight of her body
But the world is in a constant rush
And we don't have time
For anything but a cursory glance
And thus we live in a curious age
Where the things we see
With our human eyes
Are actually the illusions
While the truth lies in the invisible
When I look at you
I will consciously endeavor
To understand that your physical being
Is a tiny fraction of who you are
And in turn, please remember
That you will never truly know me
Until you get to know the invisible me

❧ Notes ❦

❧ Notes ❧

❧ Notes ❦

The New Beautiful

Strong is the new beautiful
The confident strength of a girl
Is a beautiful thing
Determination is the new beautiful
A girl's fight for her dreams
Is a beautiful thing
Positivity is the new beautiful
The radiance of optimism
Is a beautiful thing
Self-confidence is the new beautiful
Feeling good about yourself
Is a beautiful thing
Brave is the new beautiful
Standing up for what's right
Is a beautiful thing
Focus is the new beautiful
Identifying what matters to you
Is a beautiful thing
Resilience is the new beautiful
Getting up when you've been knocked down
Is a beautiful thing
Compassion is the new beautiful
Empathy for those in need
Is a beautiful thing
Creativity is the new beautiful
The ingenuity of a curious mind
Is a beautiful thing
Beautiful is the new beautiful
Defining beauty according to your own standards
Is a beautiful thing

❧ Notes ❧

❧ Notes ❦

❧ Notes ❧

Revolutionary (Just Be)

Would it be revolutionary
For us to quit caring so much
About how society defines
The ideal girl
And just be?
Would it be revolutionary
For us to reject
The stereotypical caricatures
That bombard us
Every single day
And just be?
Would it be revolutionary
For us to halt our endless quest
To fit an impossible mold
And just be?
Would it be revolutionary
If we stopped buying
What they're peddling
And just be?
Would it be revolutionary
For us to seize back our girlhood
And declare that
It was never theirs to claim
And just be?
Would it be revolutionary for us
To just be?
To just simply be?

✌ Notes ✌

❧ Notes ❧

❧ Notes ❧

Taking It Back

I'm taking it back
The power I gave away
I gave the power to someone else
To convince me that I am beautiful
I also gave them the power
To convince me
That I am not beautiful
And in doing so
I put myself at their mercy
Giving them the power
To offer validation or criticism
To fill me with confidence or insecurity
I gave them the power
To crush me or infuse me
But I'm taking it back
Because that kind of power
Is a precious thing
Not to be given away lightly
Why do we give ourselves
Away like that?
Why do we place our self worth
In the hands of another?
Making ourselves beggars
Of acceptance, love and admiration?
Whatever the reason
We must not forget
That it is never too late to reclaim it
If it was ours to give
It's ours to reclaim
And I've made my choice
I'm taking it back

❧ Notes ❧

❧ Notes ❧

❧ Notes ❦

Fickle World

A quick search will tell you
All you need to know
About the changing standards
Of this fickle world
What was beautiful in ages past
Is no longer attractive today
Current ideals of beauty
Would have been considered repulsive
In bygone days
No doubt future generations
Will look back on today's beauty trends
Perplexed by our definition of attractiveness
Because it flips and flops
With every generation
That booming voice dictating
How we must change ourselves
To accommodate the whims
Of this fickle world
But perhaps it is time
For us to declare
That is not for us to change
But for the world to change
That is not we who must acquiesce
To bow to the edicts of this fickle world
But to tell it instead
That we will no longer
Scramble to conform to its ridiculous
And ever-changing standards
And that the world itself must change
To accommodate us
As we declare that we are
Beautiful just as we are

❧ Notes ❧

❧ Notes ❦

Notes

My Someday Self

I spent years
Wishing for the future
So I could be my older self
Free to do so many more things
Able to claim my independence
And even now I look ahead
Longing for what is yet to be
Anxious to become my someday self
Always looking forward
Maybe I'll grow into a person
I will love
Maybe she will be
Everything I wish for
Perhaps she'll be admired
And maybe even adored
And so it goes
As we spend our lives
Looking forward to our someday selves
Neglecting who we are today
Thinking that we're not quite whole
Today
At this very moment
But that we're only who we want to be
Sometime far from now
It's a trap, I tell you
Daydreaming over our someday selves
So much so that we forget
We are alive right now
And who we are at this present moment
Is all we have
And all we need

✒ Notes ✒

❧ Notes ❦

❧ Notes ❧

Admit It!

Admit it!
You know there's things
You love about you
So just admit it!
Admit it to yourself
Stop feeling guilty
About feeling good
Don't let anybody make you feel
Like you should try to numb
Those sensations
Admit it!
Be brave and list them out
Celebrate them
It's totally okay
To feel totally okay about you
We don't have to
Dwell in mental sessions
Where we convince ourselves
That we should keep on looking
Until we find things about ourselves
That need fixing
You know that you are proud of yourself
For a whole list of reasons
You know that you feel good
About a host of
Physical, emotional and intellectual qualities
You recognize in yourself
So just admit it!
Don't be ashamed to admit
That you actually like who you are
Just admit it!
Admit it!

~ Notes ~

❧ Notes ❧

❧ Notes ❦

No Substitute

Some of the most beautiful plants
In the world are poisonous
And while we admire the beauty
Of such examples of life
We also behold them with caution
Understanding that poisoned perfection
Is not worth the price
And when we translate this truth
To correspond with the human experience
We know that beauty is no substitute
For so many more important things
Unparalleled physical beauty
Is no asset when paired
With an absence of compassion
The most attractive among us
Lose our admiration
When we witness a demonstration
Of their unkindness
Physical perfection is a wasted gift
When unaccompanied by a genuine heart
A dazzling smile means nothing
If it is a mask for insincerity
So when we devote a measure of time
In admiration of those we appreciate
For their physical beauty
We might also spare a moment
To observe the quality of their character
Which is a far greater indicator
Of genuine beauty
Than the way a person looks

❧ Notes ❧

Notes

❧ Notes ❧